How to Build a Happy, Healthy Downline
and Maximize Your Income

DOWNLINE DYNAMICS

Janiece C. Andrews, M.D.

PRESCRIPTIONS FOR ENLIGHTENING PATHS, INC.

**How to Build A Happy, Healthy Downline
and Maximize Your Income**

DOWNLINE DYNAMICS

**©2016 PRESCRIPTIONS FOR ENLIGHTENING PATHS
Janiece C. Andrews, MD**

Designed & Edited by Margery Phelps

Please visit our website for additional information:

http://www.howtobuildahealthydownline.com

Royalty free photographs purchased from Creative Commons.

ISBN: 978-0-9968902-3-6

Printed in the United States of America

Cherokee Rose
Publishing, LLC
INFORM. INSPIRE. ENTERTAIN.

DOWNLINE DYNAMICS

Contents

YOU ARE AWESOME !!

As an MLM business owner you are quite gutsy. You have chosen to own your business rather than trading your time for wages with limited opportunity. And that is an awesome decision.

There are hundreds of books that talk about the challenges of MLM.
They will tell you how to recruit, how to close the sale,
how to explain a pay plan. They will tell you how to dress,
what to say, and where to go.

So, why do you need another book?

Because this book is different.

This one is about **YOU** and **the real formula to YOUR success.**

When you have this formula for success, and you pass it along to your downline, then you will have **DOWNLINE DYNAMICS** – and that means you maximize your income.

Search your heart...is this what you really want?

Do you really want the formula for success?

Okay. If you answered *yes* to each question, then read on.

My Personal Thoughts and Notes

Is your energy even throughout the day?

When do you have the most energy?

Where does your energy come from?

_____

_____

_____

_____

_____

_____

_____

_____

_____

_____

_____

_____

_____

_____

_____

_____

_____

WHAT IS THE FORMULA TO SUCCESS?

The Formula to Success is not complicated and everyone can do it, but most people in business do not realize the huge impact it makes on their bottom line.

So what is the formula to success?

> **Your Personal Health + Your Personal Happiness = Your Personal Energy**

You see from our formula that the answer is *Energy.*

So, why is it that you need Energy?

To start robustly and maintain momentum, you'll need *ENERGY.*

Next, you'll need *ENERGY.*

And finally, you'll need *ENERGY.*

Does this mean that having courage is not important?

Does this mean that having determination is not important?

Does this mean that having a good *why* is not important?

No. You need all that and more.

Yet none of that goes quite far enough without *ENERGY.*

My Personal Thoughts and Notes

How do you know when you are well hydrated?

How do you know when you are in need of water?

Do you feel the same after a meal of processed food as after a meal of whole foods?

_____

_____

_____

_____

_____

_____

_____

_____

_____

_____

_____

_____

_____

_____

_____

_____

_____

_____

_____

_____

_____

HOW DO WE GET ENERGY?

1:   NUTRITION

We get energy from the foods we eat. There are basic rules that apply when we trust our bodies to convert the food we consume into energy. Each of our 37 trillion cells has an energy factory rearing to go into production to generate energy for us. Since that is a fact of biology and a given we can rely upon, then there are things we need to do to support that apparatus whenever possible:

Drink great water that is alkalinized and preferably restructured to ensure it hydrates your cells; the recommended volume to consume is ½ your body weight daily in ounces – more on humid days.

Eat food that is alive and un-radiated. This way, the enzymes can be used by your body to make the amino acids available to build proteins.

Eat whole foods that preserve vitamin and mineral content that your body can utilize to build new muscles, nerves, etc.

Eat processed food rarely so your energy-making apparatus will make fuel for you to use rather than try to discard or store byproducts of the processed food.

Eat your last meal at least 3 hours before going to bed to avoid the discomforts of indigestion.

Break your overnight fast with a breakfast; eating protein as early as 20 minutes after awakening ensures balanced blood sugar levels throughout the day and good appetite control.

My Personal Thoughts and Notes

How much sleep do you actually need to function at your best?

When you are unable to sleep throughout the night do you know why?

What are ways you ensure sound sweet sleep?

_____

_____

_____

_____

_____

_____

_____

_____

_____

_____

_____

_____

_____

_____

_____

_____

_____

HOW DO WE GET ENERGY?

2:   SLEEP

Know the amount of sleep you need to function at your best.

Do your best to establish a regular bedtime so that your body benefits from the non-REM (deep sleep) stages where the body mends itself, and REM sleep where the mind integrates previous learning.

As much as possible avoid alcohol, nicotine, and prescribed or over-the-counter (OTC) sleep drugs at bedtime. They can backfire and cause unpredictable awakenings.

Practice prayer, meditation, and relaxation techniques to preserve normal sleep structure.

My Personal Thoughts and Notes

At what time in the 24-hr cycle does exercise support balanced energy (or balance in your energy)?

What type of exercise is the most energizing for your entire body?

What type of exercise energizes your mind?

_____

_____

_____

_____

_____

_____

_____

_____

_____

_____

_____

_____

_____

_____

_____

_____

HOW DO WE GET ENERGY?

3: EXERCISE

Check with your healthcare provider regarding the best type and amount of exercise for you and make a commitment to do it.

Proper exercise supports your immune system, metabolism, emotional balance, food utilization and fuel (energy) production.

The previous discussion outlines the types of energy with which we are already familiar. You cannot survive without observing these laws on energy. Make protecting yourself from energy loss a personal goal.

Before going further about generating energy, it's useful to know about the common **energy zappers**. In this way you can recognize them and avoid or minimize their impact on you.

My Personal Thoughts and Notes

How do you know when your energy is zapped?

What do you do to recover your zapped energy?

What are at least 2 ways you prevent your energy from being zapped?

_____

_____

_____

_____

_____

_____

_____

_____

_____

_____

_____

_____

_____

_____

_____

_____

_____

ENERGY ZAPPERS

Electromagnetic fields (EMF) and electromagnetic radiation (EMR):

- Appliances
- Computers
- Cell Phones
- Televisions
- Microwave Ovens
- Chaotic Electricity
- Cordless Phones
- Solar Flares
- Radiation

Emotional Factors

- Fear
- Anger
- Unforgiveness
- Anxiety
- Worry
- Depression
- Disappointments
- Negative Self-Talk
- Procrastination
- Jealousy
- Resentment
- Hatred
- Grudges

Health Factors

- Toxicity — Foods contaminated with pesticides
  Draining relationships and unhappy people
  Unresolved conflicts
- Malnutrition — Consuming foods with low nutritional value
- Constipation — When bowels move less frequently than 1 to 2 times daily
- Hormones — Get annual thyroid checks – especially if you use fluoride toothpaste or shower in unfiltered water.
- Dental Disease — Root canals, silver amalgams
- Allergies — Overworked immune response; fatigue is a by-product
- Chronic Disease — Being sick utilizes much energy. Establish a coaching relationship with your health provider to prevent disease.
- Lack of Exercise — Slows metabolism and leads to weight gain and poor sleep.

My Personal Thoughts and Notes

When does it seem like energy is stuck in your body?

In what ways do your thoughts affect your energy?

How can other people's opinions affect your energy?

_____

_____

_____

_____

_____

_____

_____

_____

_____

_____

_____

_____

_____

_____

_____

_____

_____

SO, IS THERE ANOTHER KIND OF ENERGY?

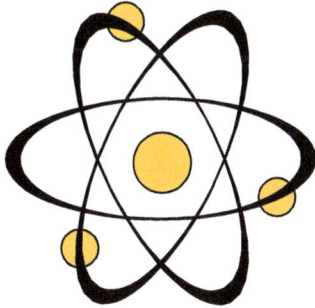

Yes, there is another kind of energy called **Energy Psychology** (EP). To understand it we must tap into some background information before entering this exciting domain. How, you may wonder, does Energy Psychology differ from Psychology? To answer that let's look at the following:

Only now is the field of biology beginning to update their understanding of how the human body really functions based on the principles of quantum physics [1]. The implications are proving to be at least as astounding as what the high tech revolutions have already brought.

The basic premise behind energy psychology is that our **negative thoughts, beliefs, and emotions** (which are energy) can get stuck in the body and clog up the natural flow of energy. This stuck energy (trapped emotion) is the cause of most emotional and physical pain as well as disease.

Psychology deals with this problem by helping you gain insight into the causes of your emotional difficulties and assists you in changing your behaviors. However, you are left needing to use your will power to try to behave in these new healthier ways. You still feel the internal urges in your *gut* to behave the old way. The result is an ongoing internal struggle between your gut feelings and your will power. This is very hard and progress can be very expensive and slow, sometimes taking years or even never.

On the other hand, EP leads the way into 21st century psychotherapy, provides rapid, reliable and lasting treatment of a broadening range of psychological issues by applying some of the understandings of quantum physics to *SUPERCHARGE* the process of *psychotherapeutic change and assist people in developing their **Intentional Effectiveness***.

A simplified way to think of EP procedures is to view them as ***acupuncture for the emotions, but without the needles***. These methods have already been applauded by self-help gurus **Wayne Dyer** and **Tony Robbins**, self-esteem expert **Nathaniel Brandon**, renowned physicists like **William Tiller**, and best-selling microbiologist **Candace Pert** [2].

My Personal Thoughts and Notes

When have you tried your hardest to achieve a goal only to fall short of it?

When have you encountered an unsuccessful outcome that was very similar to a prior unsuccessful outcome?

What do these outcomes have in common?

_____

_____

_____

_____

_____

_____

_____

_____

_____

_____

_____

_____

_____

_____

_____

_____

_____

WHAT DO I HAVE TO DO?

The great achievers in the MLM industry, Zig Ziglar, Myron Golden, John Assaraf, Jerry Clark, Jeffery Combs, and Jim Rohn inspire you to achieve a level beyond horizons…because you can. They tell you how to do it, and they make great examples of how <u>not</u> to do it.

This is both insightful and inspiring, yet may be insufficient to motivate many people who have ambition and dreams. The goal to **_avoid being something_** lacks the voltage to pull or propel an individual away from his/her current and past pain.

Why? Because the emotion is stuck in the energy system called Meridians. It's not a simple matter of will power in most cases.

❖ When you understand this, you can lead your members who flounder and have excuse-after-excuse for failing to follow through.

❖ When you understand this, you can lead your members who seem to attract one unfortunate circumstance after another in their quest to get away from a lesser economic status.

❖ When you understand this you can lead that team member who takes one step forward and two backwards.

I've seen great leaders in various MLM organizations who have super *whys* (move-aways) and so much great physical energy they can light up an auditorium! Yet they are not reaching their goals; they are not expressing their potential.

Why? Largely because they have unconscious sabotaging beliefs that got registered in their energy system at the time the pain struck–usually in childhood. Haven't you known of a situation where a kid from a highly disorganized family structure vows he'll never live or be like that; but he grows up to be just like that–the thing he hated so much?

Another common example is a girl who came from a home where the father was an abusive alcoholic, which she hated and from which she escaped, only to marry at least one abusive alcoholic husband in adulthood. So pain, in and of itself, may or may not serve sufficiently to motivate change. In both cases, the individual's feelings of aversion were stuck in their cells and the feelings, being charged energy forms, attracted *in kind* since the energy was never neutralized. (See *The Secret, The Law of Attraction*)[3.]

My Personal Thoughts and Notes

What beliefs do you have that are likely holding your back?

How can you tell when you have a toxic belief?

Have you ever been so comfortable in life that you were afraid to make a change that may or may not benefit you?

_____

_____

_____

_____

_____

_____

_____

_____

_____

_____

_____

_____

_____

_____

_____

_____

WHY SABOTAGING BELIEFS ARE TOXIC

Sabotaging beliefs can undermine change because they serve as a **resistance**.

Our subconscious mind wants to keep us safe and is very resistant to change. So, even if the possibility of change consciously feels exciting and new, the subconscious will probably do its utmost to keep us firmly rooted where we are now, because *now* is safe and familiar.

There is a pay-off for the subconscious to hold on to the familiar and this is known as **Secondary Benefit Syndrome**. In other words, there is some benefit to staying where we are now even if consciously we desire to move forward. And this can greatly diminish our Happiness.

Don't despair; there is something that can be done about giant, sabotaging beliefs.

My Personal Thoughts and Notes

Would you prefer a long extensive process to reduce uncomfortable psychological tensions to one that is brief and at least as effective?

What do you know of acupuncture?

Have you ever had acupuncture treatment?

_____

_____

_____

_____

_____

_____

_____

_____

_____

_____

_____

_____

_____

_____

_____

_____

_____

_____

OVERCOMING SUBCONSCIOUS RESISTANCE TO CHANGE

EMOTIONAL FREEDOM TECHNIQUE

Emotional Freedom Technique (EFT) is a therapy with origins in ancient Chinese medicine. It is a tapping technique that works on the body's energy systems, and was developed by Gary Craig, a Stanford trained Engineer and Ordained Minister, following Dr. Roger Callahan's discovery that energy imbalances can have profound affects on personal psychology.

EFT is 5 to 10 to 20 times faster than other methods.

EFT has been known to only take weeks or months to get relief and experience deep healing, instead of months to years (or never) with traditional psychotherapy.

EFT uses gentle tapping on the acupoints of the body's meridian system (the body's energy pathways) to change the way energy travels through the body. During tapping, small shock waves are sent through the energy system, which stimulate smooth flow and clear blockages.

In short, EFT works like acupuncture but without the needles.

For a **FREE MERIDIAN CHART**, visit
The Association for Meridian Energy Therapies'
website at http://theamt.com

For a **FREE TAPPING GUIDE**,
visit http://eft.mercola.com

My Personal Thoughts and Notes

Could you locate the tapping points on your body?

Apply different pressures to the points and see what if anything you notice.

Describe what you notice.

_____

_____

_____

_____

_____

_____

_____

_____

_____

_____

_____

_____

_____

_____

_____

_____

_____

EFT TAPPING POINTS

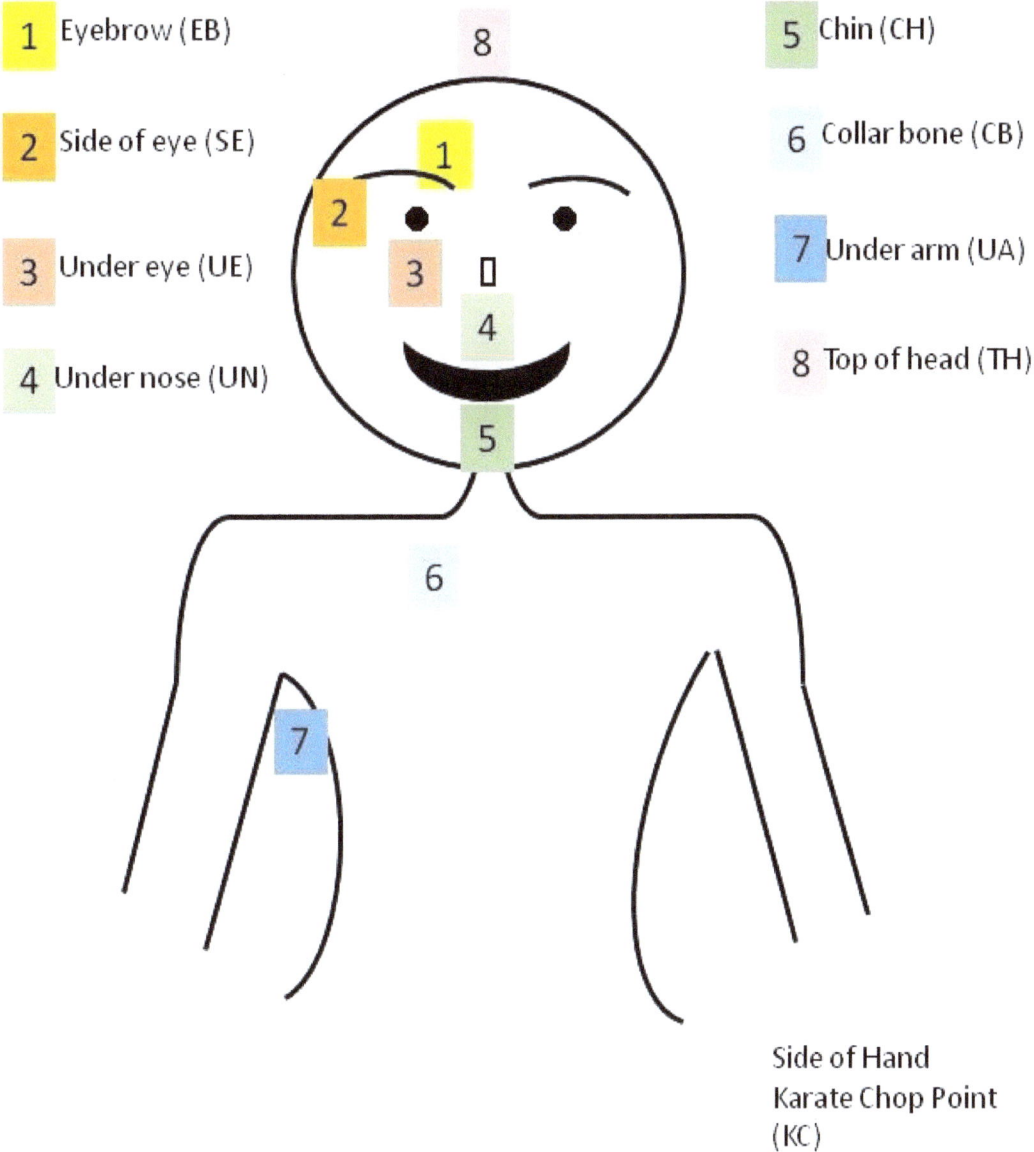

1 Eyebrow (EB)

2 Side of eye (SE)

3 Under eye (UE)

4 Under nose (UN)

8

1

2

3

4

5

6

7

5 Chin (CH)

6 Collar bone (CB)

7 Under arm (UA)

8 Top of head (TH)

Side of Hand
Karate Chop Point
(KC)

EFT DIAGRAM
©Janiece Andrews, MD
and Margery Phelps

My Personal Thoughts and Notes

What do you think you would feel when the root cause of a problem is eliminated?

What makes EFT so easy?

How easy is it to *tune into* negative feelings?

_____

_____

_____

_____

_____

_____

_____

_____

_____

_____

_____

_____

_____

_____

_____

_____

_____

_____

_____

EMOTIONAL FREEDOM TECHNIQUE

EFT not only helps to release negative emotions, it can also help you to see how unreal your thoughts are and how quickly they can change or disappear. This is a great technique to get you closer to being in the *Here and Now*, which means being fully present in the moment.

The speed and effectiveness of EFT is the result of treating the problem at its source. Stressful and traumatic experiences cause disruptions or imbalances in the body's energy system, and these result in the experience of negative emotions. Once these imbalances are corrected, the negative emotions are released and shifted into positive emotions.

EFT does this by having you *tune into* the negative emotion, tap on energy meridians, and perform other energy balancing exercises to help the mind/body heal itself. This powerful approach often quickly resolves emotional distress, as well as frequently removes many physical complaints.

Luckily, with EFT we have a tool which can override the stubborn subconscious. To assist my clients in overcoming that resistance, I usually suggest tapping on the karate chop point (KC) and repeat the following three times:

> *Even though for whatever reason, there's a part of me*
> *that doesn't want to let go of this _____*
> *[illness, weight, lack of money, anger, etc],*
> *there's a bigger part of me that wants to accept myself.*

The purpose of this is to neutralize the *Secondary Benefit Syndrome* (Kenny, 2004). Once this is cleared, we are ready to apply regular EFT on the issue at hand.

When we tap on our limiting beliefs, traumatic memories, or pain, we shift our perspective, gently allowing our subconscious to consider change. Once the subconscious realizes there is nothing to gain from holding on to the problem, it is open to changing.

CHANGE
your thoughts & you
CHANGE
your world.
Norman Vincent Peale

My Personal Thoughts and Notes

Why is EFT considered more effective than standard and alternative therapies?

What are some direct benefits to having root causes eliminated?

How might EFT be useful to you? To someone you love?

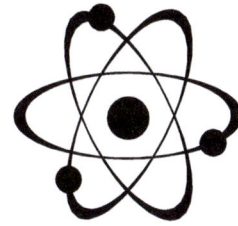

BENEFITS OF EFT

- ❖ EFT focuses on energy patterns in the body and often works where standard and even alternative therapies don't.

- ❖ This simple tool gives gentle and long-lasting relief.

- ❖ No drugs or special equipment needed.

- ❖ Anyone can quickly learn EFT, even over the telephone.

- ❖ The tapping doesn't have to be done "perfectly" to work.

- ❖ There is no minimum or maximum amount of tapping.

- ❖ You can tap as little or as often as you want.

- ❖ Emotional problems, as well as physical problems, can be alleviated.

- ❖ You don't even have to believe in this technique in order for it to work.

My Personal Thoughts and Notes

What is the EFT recipe?

Is there a difference between what you think and what you feel?

What is one difference?

How important is it to know the difference?

_____

_____

_____

_____

_____

_____

_____

_____

_____

_____

_____

_____

_____

_____

_____

_____

_____

THE EFT "RECIPE" – HOW DO I DO THIS?

In a nutshell, EFT begins with **stating the problem**.

Let's say, for example, you are a negative thinker or negative person. (Negative or doubtful thinking can kill an idea before it even gets off the ground. Want to reach your goals faster? Start thinking more positively...now!)

To get a numerical evaluation on your problem, measure it on a scale of 0 to 10, with 10 being the most true, by asking yourself, "How true does it feel?"

Make sure you ask yourself what you *feel* not what you *think.*

It's much harder to 'plug' into the issue when we are in our head. Feelings bring us into our body and connect us to our intuition. Here is a stellar example for you:

A client of mine is an MLM leader and reported an amazing experience with one of his Downline Associates, whom he was coaching. My client was adept at applying EFT and tapped daily. He detected issues of procrastination in Mel and applied coaching skills to learn the following:

A REAL LIFE CASE STUDY

Mel, a 47 year old married male, is a college graduate who majored in Business Administration and minored in Marketing. He found that his job security was not guaranteed, even after being employed by five financial services companies, including a Fortune 500 firm. His health was quite good and he exercised regularly.

Mel, being forced to work several part time jobs, each without benefits, entered the world of multi-level marketing because he understood business and application of the principles. His wife Pam, a nurse, worked evenings so she could be home in the day with their three children ages 3 to 9, and family benefits came from Pam's job.

Before Mel's last job layoff, they purchased their dream home, in just the right community, in the ideal school district. Pam fully supported Mel's home business endeavors and went to rallies with him and hosted trainings and "Coreings."

My Personal Thoughts and Notes

Could you identify with Mel's enthusiasm and motivation?

Are you challenged to participate fully in business-growing activities?

Can you sometimes feel/see the glow of achieving the vision yet doubts pop up?

_____

_____

_____

_____

_____

_____

_____

_____

_____

_____

_____

_____

_____

_____

_____

A Case Study

Mel was attracted to and challenged by direct sales. Multilevel marketing appealed to his sense of fairness and enterprise and he was meticulous in gathering background information and as many details as he could before launching into a business.

He took advantage of all the product, sales, marketing, and prospecting training that was offered by the companies. Yet, something seemed to stop him from sustained success. On the surface he appeared to attract people who had an interest in the benefits he presented and he rapidly grew MLM businesses into large organizations.

Mel motivated his downline to attend conventions and local events, and from the outside he was successful. The businesses had great compensation plans and usually were considered ground floor opportunities. He always saw himself as a good salesman with greater than average leadership abilities and exceptional people skills.

However, Mel was greatly disheartened by his family's attitude toward his entrepreneur activities and constantly compared him to his siblings who had "real jobs." They thought he was not applying himself to the job market. His primary goal was to prove to his family that he could be a success.

It became more difficult as he watched his third lucrative opportunity dwindle away, this time in a communication company; it was the second time this had happened when he was at the crest of reaching high earnings. Simultaneously, financial needs arose – braces for the children, emergency room visits, car troubles, and a basement flood. Uncontrollable events drained the family of any money reserves they had in the bank.

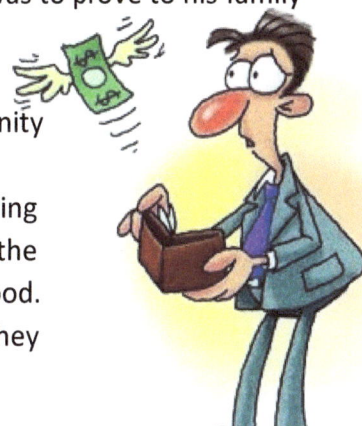

Meanwhile, his marriage was under strain. Pam worked longer hours but wanted to be at home for the children. She couldn't understand how Mel could build his business quickly, only to have people drop out of his down lines when he got to a point where his income could double or escalate. Each story was similar. Pam noticed that he slacked off making cold and warm calls and his attendance to the local meetings became irregular. When his checks got smaller, he blamed his group. There seemed to be a pattern.

My Personal Thoughts and Notes

Do you endorse words or descriptions of yourself that may or may not actually be true?

Do you believe that your thoughts are entirely your own?

What percentage of your thoughts may not be entirely your own?

Case Study ...

Mel had been taught that it was selfish to want more than he needed. Mel's father told him that he wasn't to come back from college with *a big head,* and that he, the father, *was still the boss and in charge.* Paying the bills and having enough was safe, as was keeping a savings account for *a rainy day.*

From his mother Mel heard that getting a good job was the ultimate achievement, and staying at one place until retirement was ideal. She also made negative comments on news reports about wealthy people, saying "rich people are greedy and selfish."

Pam noticed that Mel exhibited highs and lows and wondered if he was causing his organization to dwindle off. They finally sat down and talked about their situation, the strain on their marriage, and her observations.

Mel felt so defeated, and in that state he confided that he was *stuck* and had been for years, being caught between two worlds. On one hand he wanted to meet his obligations to his family; on the other, he wanted to please his parents and not lose their love.

So what was the outcome? Total dissatisfaction and lack of fulfillment.

Pam talked him into couples counseling to improve their marriage. She had heard of Brief Treatment of Stress-related conditions from a co-worker who had great success and they made an appointment.

The therapist talked with each one individually after the initial appointment, and in short order observed some issues in Mel's belief system that were actually sabotaging his success— issues that would allow him to approach success but not go all the way to lasting rewards for his efforts.

These beliefs so thoroughly *sapped his energy* that he was no longer an inspiration to his team. He became a MLM Leader without steam and it showed.

She explained that his beliefs generated vibrations, as all thoughts do, and because of the indiscriminate nature of the *laws of attraction,* what he was attracting matched his own vibrations.

The therapist told Mel about the Meridian system of energy, and how beliefs and thoughts either move through them or get stuck and create undesired outcomes. Changing it, however, was as simple as 1-2-3! He was very encouraged and curious about his obstructing beliefs.

My Personal Thoughts and Notes

How can you tell if what you think are your thoughts?

What difference does it make if what you think the majority of the time doesn't belong to you?

Name one or more sources that influence what you think of yourself.

_____

_____

_____

_____

_____

_____

_____

_____

_____

_____

_____

_____

_____

_____

_____

What the therapist found were beliefs that stopped him dead in his tracks.

- If I succeed, people will expect me to succeed at everything I do

- Success is too hard

- Rich people are greedy

- If I am successful, I will lose my family (time, closeness, divorce)

- I'm not smart enough, good enough. . .

- People will judge me

- People will be jealous of me

Mel was unconsciously sabotaging his success; if his income was not too grand, then he would not stand out, and therefore avoid being a threat to his father. His subconscious fear was that he would lose his family, or they would be jealous of him—or that his mother might think (judge) he was greedy like rich people.

Like his father, Mel kept money in the bank, which paid little interest, even though he understood the stock market and how to select stocks for greater returns on his dollars. Instead he kept money in a low earnings Mutual Fund account.

Poor   Rich

My Personal Thoughts and Notes

What is the EFT "set-up" phrase?

What is an affirmation?

What is the importance of the "truth statement?"

_____

_____

_____

_____

_____

_____

_____

_____

_____

_____

_____

_____

_____

_____

_____

_____

_____

THE EFT SESSIONS

Round 1: The Problem - EFT Set-up Statement: HOOK-UP

While saying the following "Set-up Phrase," tap the Karate Chop (KC) point, using the fingers of one hand to tap onto the KC of the opposite hand.   Two to four fingers may be engaged in tapping. The "Set-up Phrase" should state the problem to be addressed along with an affirmation. (In our example, we will use statements and questions that would be appropriate for Mel. Of course, you should use statements and questions that are applicable to you.)

1. Even though I fear that I will lose the love of my father, I deeply and completely accept myself.

2. Even though I fear losing my family's love, I deeply and completely accept myself.

3. Even though I am afraid people will judge me and think I am greedy if I have plenty of money , I deeply and completely accept myself.

Repeat each phrase in the set-up 3 times. Take 2 deep belly breaths in through the nose and out through the mouth and relax a minute before moving to the tapping points. Then at the tapping points (see diaphragm) on each spot, tap about seven times at each spot while stating a reminder of the problem, such as:

I Fear   *I'll lose my father's love;*
afraid people will judge me;
people will think I'm greedy.

Tap all of the points while repeating this reminder phrase, addressing specific aspects of the problem as needed until your TRUTH level is down. If the level is not as near to zero as you would like, repeat the EFT process.

My Personal Thoughts and Notes

What is a "belly breath?"

How useful is it?

Perform 3 "belly breaths" and note what you feel and where you feel it.

_____

_____

_____

_____

_____

_____

_____

_____

_____

_____

_____

_____

_____

_____

_____

_____

_____

_____

EFT Sequence

TH – I'm afraid I will lose the love of my father.

EB – How can I stand to lose his love?

SE – What if I lose my family's love?

UE – What would I do if I lost their love?

UN – How can I be successful without their love?

CH – What if I never get it back?

CB – I fear they will never get over it.

UA – What if I can't make it if they don't get over it?

Take a deep breath, roll your shoulders and wiggle your toes.

Check your 0-10 Truth Statement level, "I'm afraid that I will lose the love of my father," "I'm afraid I'll lose my family's love."

There is no right or wrong answer. The level may have gone down, stayed the same, or even have gone up. It's not unusual for it to go up at this point.

Just make a note of how true the statement **feels** to you after the first EFT tapping round.

The intensity level of the truth statement will be more accurate if you plug into how it feels in your body, instead of what you think in your head.

My Personal Thoughts and Notes

Would there be value to you to include "belly-breath-breaks" into your day?

What is 1 possible benefit?

How does it feel to take a belly breath, roll your shoulders, stretch your neck and wiggle your toes?

_____

_____

_____

_____

_____

_____

_____

_____

_____

_____

_____

_____

_____

_____

_____

_____

_____

Round 2: The Turn-around: REFRAME

EFT Setup Statements

> KC – Even though I feel like I can't do anything to please them, I deeply and completely love, accept and respect myself.

> KC – Even though some of them may think I'm greedy, I deeply and completely love, accept and respect myself.

> KC – Even though I sometimes want to give up, I deeply and completely love, accept and respect myself.

EFT Sequence

> TH – Sometimes it feels like I can't do anything to please them.

> EB – Sometimes it feels as if I'm wasting my time.

> SE – I fear that this is too hard for me.

> UE – I want my business to be successful.

> UN – I'm afraid that people will think I am greedy.

> CH – I'm afraid I'll lose my family's love because they think I am greedy.

> CB – I'm afraid they'll judge me.

> UA - Sometimes I want to give up, but I know I must keep on going.

Take a deep breath, roll your shoulders, stretch your neck and wiggle your toes.

Check your 1-10 Truth Statement level, "I'm afraid I can't do anything to please them."

My Personal Thoughts and Notes

Is there an area of your life where you clearly know that you're capable of doing better than you currently are?

Do you sometimes struggle with taking action even though you realize it is in your best interest to do so?

Have you ever felt like giving up?

_____

_____

_____

_____

_____

_____

_____

_____

_____

_____

_____

_____

_____

_____

_____

_____

_____

_____

Round 3: Affirm and Appreciate (No Setup)

EFT Sequence

TH – If they judge me wrong, I'm still an awesome person.

EB – I will celebrate even my smallest steps to success.

SE – When I think about giving up, I'll just take a deep breath
and keep on going.

UE – Many successful people lacked the support of loved ones;
I'll just use them as role models!

UN – I will not accept failure.

CH – Somebody's opinion of me, real or imagined, is not my business.

CB – I will not be intimidated by the opinions of others.

UA – Small successes will build my belief in myself.

I Believe

Take a deep breath, roll your shoulders and wiggle your toes.

Check your 0-10 Truth Statement level, "I'm afraid they will judge me wrong."

How does it feel now? Compare this to your initial level.

Even if the level of your truth statement feels like it only went down a little, *shifts in
the way you think, feel and act in regard to this change will begin to take place.*

My Personal Thoughts and Notes

Have you put off making necessary changes because you thought that they were too difficult to achieve?

Have you been really hopeful about making necessary changes just to have your enthusiasm fizzle out?

Can using EFT change that pattern?

_____

_____

_____

_____

_____

_____

_____

_____

_____

_____

_____

_____

_____

_____

_____

_____

_____

The Case Study Outcome

The therapist reported that Mel's outcome was quite remarkable after the first session. He continued with daily tapping, and within three weeks new members were joining his organization and existing members were staying in. His relationship with his wife and children improved as he had more time to spend with them and enjoy his new comfort with being successful.

The roadblock of beliefs that he would be poorly judged for succeeding were removed and, true to the law of attraction, his momentum grew and so did his organization, and no one spoke of dropping out. In fact, they were motivated to reach for new challenges and achieve higher and higher levels of success.

My Personal Thoughts and Notes

_____

_____

_____

_____

_____

_____

_____

_____

_____

_____

_____

_____

_____

_____

_____

_____

_____

_____

EFT has been proven successful in thousands of clinical cases. It can be applied to just about every problem you can name and it often works *where nothing else will.*

- It addresses the negative thought/emotion you are focusing on *at its source.*

- It resets the subtle energy in the body's meridians and neutralizes the negativity.

- It causes the release of natural endorphins and neurotransmitters such as Serotonin.

Essentially, EFT short circuits the mind-body connection that's going on between the thoughts, emotions, and sabotaging beliefs operating in the energy system. How energetically cool is that?

You can learn all the basics from its founder Gary Craig by downloading the Free EFT Starter Manual from the official EFT website: www.emofree.com.

I hope you have enjoyed **Downline Dynamics**, but please, don't wait for your downline to disappear before you get help.

Call me today and get your MLM business on the road to success with a complimentary consultation for you, and to schedule a webinar for your downline. Together we can make a world of difference in your life, your finances, and your dreams.

You can reach me at drjanieceandrews@msn.com

Our website is: http://www.howtobuildahealthydownline.com

My Personal Thoughts and Notes

_____

_____

_____

_____

_____

_____

_____

_____

_____

_____

_____

_____

_____

_____

_____

_____

_____

_____

_____

ABOUT THE AUTHOR - Janiece C. Andrews, M.D.

Prescriptions For Enlightening Paths, Inc. (PEP) is the parent of PEP Solutions, our educational service unit. Janiece C. Andrews, M.D., Board Certified Psychiatrist with specialties in Child & Adolescent Psychiatry, BioEnergetics, Psychosomatic and Integrative Medicine, is the Medical Director. Her approach since the 70s has been Holistic, which has applications today. PEP integrates effective treatment modalities in order for our patients to achieve the highest standard of physical, emotional, mental, and spiritual health.

The Paradigm Shift Has Occurred

Always on the frontiers of change, and upon recognizing the most recent paradigm shift in medicine, Dr. Andrews has extended her studies and borders to be responsive to the needs and expectations of her patients. "They are looking for real answers and for ways to take charge of their health."

The PEP series, and its transformational approach to ultimate wellness and personal well-being, was the result of her vision. PEP encompasses a wide variety of services and products designed to help individuals "recognize and utilize their unlimited potential."

My Mission Statement

As a physician, my mission is to focus on providing credible, verifiable information that has demonstrated potential to reduce and/or reverse the occurrence of chronic illness and its negative impact on consumers of health care. This shall be conducted in a responsible and ethical manner such that the consumer is empowered with the tools required to acquire and maintain optimal physical, mental, emotional and spiritual well-being. Our services come without 'fine print disclaimers' or warnings of serious side effects — just information presented in a clear respectful manner.

We Are a Catalyst for Transformation

It is my desire to be a catalyst for transformation of thought as new light is shone on old subjects. Lack of tools to navigate life's basic challenges has been the basis for much suffering. Personal well-being and development can only be enhanced as a result of the focus on preventive medicine and the paradigm shift. When taken to its most common denominator, the translation is that "prevention is preferable to cure." This approach results in a most desirable extension of health spans and a narrowing of the gap between life and health spans.

My Commitment to You

My commitment is to facilitate your successful navigation through the maze of scientific information that may appear contradictory at times. A network of collaborating colleagues enriches my resources and brings more benefit to you. By way of integrating allopathic, functional and alternative medicine principles, a holistic approach to meeting the requirements of our patients is created, an added benefit.

Your Reliable and Trusted Resource for Information

Furthermore, it is my intention to be established as a reliable and trusted resource of information from which you may build a framework for organizing and sorting the often-times contradictory and confusing health/scientific information and printed media that floods the airways and marketplace daily.

My goal is to form partnerships with our patients and create treatment plans that address the challenges to their achievement of optimal health and wellness. In turn they may collaborate with their primary medical care team, forming an in-depth shared partnership.

To schedule *Downline Dynamics* Training
for your organization,
please contact Dr. Andrews at 717-303-0505
or e-mail at: drjanieceandrews@msn.com.

ENDNOTES and WORKS CITED

[1] Lipton, Bruce H. *The Biology of Belief: Unleashing the Power of Consciousness, Matter, and Miracles*. Santa Rosa, CA: Mountain of Love/Elite, 2005. Print.

[2] Feinstein, David, Donna Eden, and Gary Craig. *The Promise of Energy Psychology: Revolutionary Tools for Dramatic Personal Change*. Ashland, OR: Innersource, 2007. Print.

[3] *The Secret*. Prod. Rhonda Byrne. 2006. DVD

Kenny, Lindsay. *EFT Reversals*. Out Front Productions, LLC. 2004

Nauman, Karen. "EFT Tapping Points: What Emotion Connects to Each Tapping Point?" *TapIntoEFT.com*. Web.

www.ingramcontent.com/pod-product-compliance
Lightning Source LLC
Chambersburg PA
CBHW052043190326
41520CB00002BA/169